NUBIAN KINGDOM

Kushite Empire
(EGYPTIAN HISTORY)

ANCIENT HISTORY FOR KIDS
5TH GRADE SOCIAL STUDIES

BABY PROFESSOR
EDUCATION KIDS

In this book, we're going to talk about the Nubian Kingdom. So, let's get right to it!

THE ANCIENT KINGDOM OF KUSH

The Kingdom of Kush, also called Nubia, was one of the first civilizations that formed in the valley of the Nile River in the northeastern section of Africa. The kingdom was south of the Egyptian civilization and was constructed at the foot of the mountains, the source of the River Nile. It was established around 2000 BC.

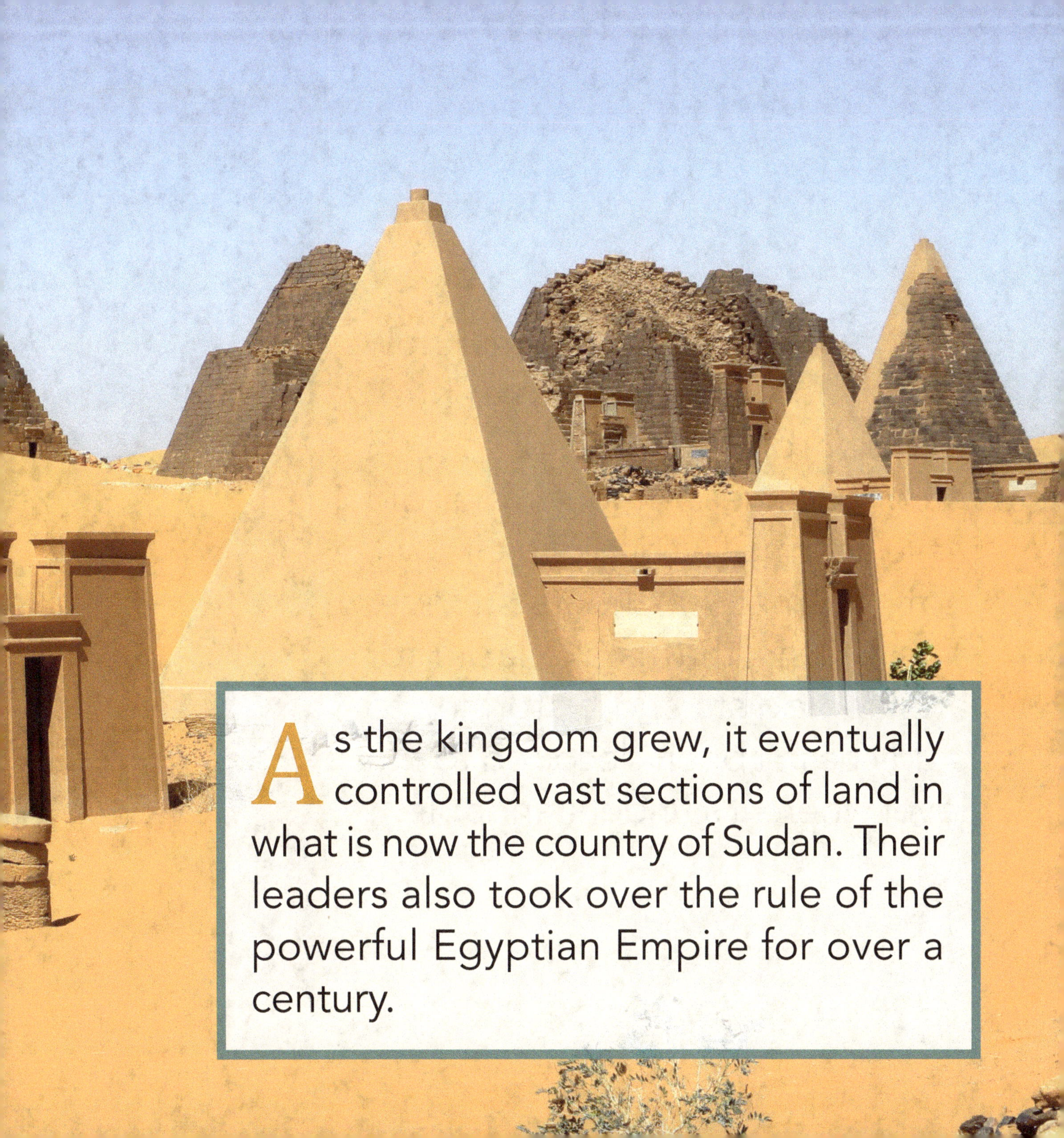

As the kingdom grew, it eventually controlled vast sections of land in what is now the country of Sudan. Their leaders also took over the rule of the powerful Egyptian Empire for over a century.

Much of what historians know about the kingdom of Kush comes from writing sources in other countries. Although they did have a form of writing of their own, not too many artifacts survive. The writing that is available for archaeologists and historians to study hasn't been decoded to the level where it's understandable.

The written sources from Ancient Egypt and Ancient Rome indicate that the Kush Kingdom existed before the civilization of Egypt. The Kush Empire extended from the

Mediterranean Sea to past the sixth cataract of the Nile River. A cataract is an area in the river where there are large boulders so the water is shallow.

THE LAND OF GOLD

The Egyptians called their neighbors in the land located south of them, "Nubians" from the Egyptian word for gold metal. The Kingdom of Kush had gold in abundance. The Nubians also had vast resources of iron ore, which was very important for the manufacture of weapons. These two resources made the kingdom very prosperous.

VIEW OF NUBIAN VILLAGE

The Nubians were important trading partners and they traded with Egypt as well as other African kingdoms. They also traded with civilizations in the lands we now know as the Middle East. The Nubians traded their precious metals for ivory and pelts from animals. They also traded for pottery.

FARMING IN THE KINGDOM OF KUSH

Because the kingdom was located at the start of the Nile River, it had good fertile soil that was available for farming. It didn't depend on the seasonal Egyptian flooding of the Nile. The kingdom had a good quantity of rainfall as well. However, the population soon outgrew their food sources.

The Kushite merchants frequently exchanged their precious metals for food and drink such as olives, olive oil, and wine from the Greeks. They also traded for Egyptian papyrus, which had a multitude of uses.

A BRIEF HISTORY OF KUSH

Most of the population of Kush was located in three different cities.

- Kerma, which was located near the third cataract of the Nile

- Napata, which was the capital city for many years, a major trading hub, and a burial region, and was located near the fourth cataract
- Meroë, which became the capital in 591 BC

STONE HEAD OF THUTMOSE I

The Kingdom of Kush was, at different times in history, friendly with the Egyptians and at other times they were Egypt's enemies. As their northern neighbor expanded, around 1500 BC, the Egyptian Pharaoh Thutmose I decided to take the Kingdom of Kush and make it part of Egypt.

The Nubians were part of the Egyptian culture for about 770 years, then circa 730 BC, a powerful Nubian king by the name of Piye overthrew the government of Egypt. He conquered the entire valley of the Nile River and became the 25th Dynasty's Pharaoh. He was the first of the "Black Pharaohs." His Nubian warriors were known for their expertise with bows and arrows and Nubia was known as the "Land of the Bow."

Piye reigned as Pharaoh of Egypt from around 744 BC to 714 BC. Even though he had returned to his homeland in Nubia after he became Pharaoh, he wanted to be entombed in the classic Egyptian way. He was buried in a pyramid. It had been five centuries since any pharaohs had been buried in this style.

The 25th Dynasty lasted for about 75 years. However, it ended in chaos. The Assyrians overthrew the region and expelled the Nubians

from power. The new rulers destroyed statues and other monuments that depicted the black pharaohs. They tried to erase them from history.

PSAMTEK II STATUE

After they were defeated, the Nubians escaped to the capital city of Napata. However, they were pushed even further south when Psamtek II, the pharaoh of the 26th Dynasty destroyed the city of Napata. At that point, the Nubians moved the capital city to Meroë. Their new location had been strategically thought out.

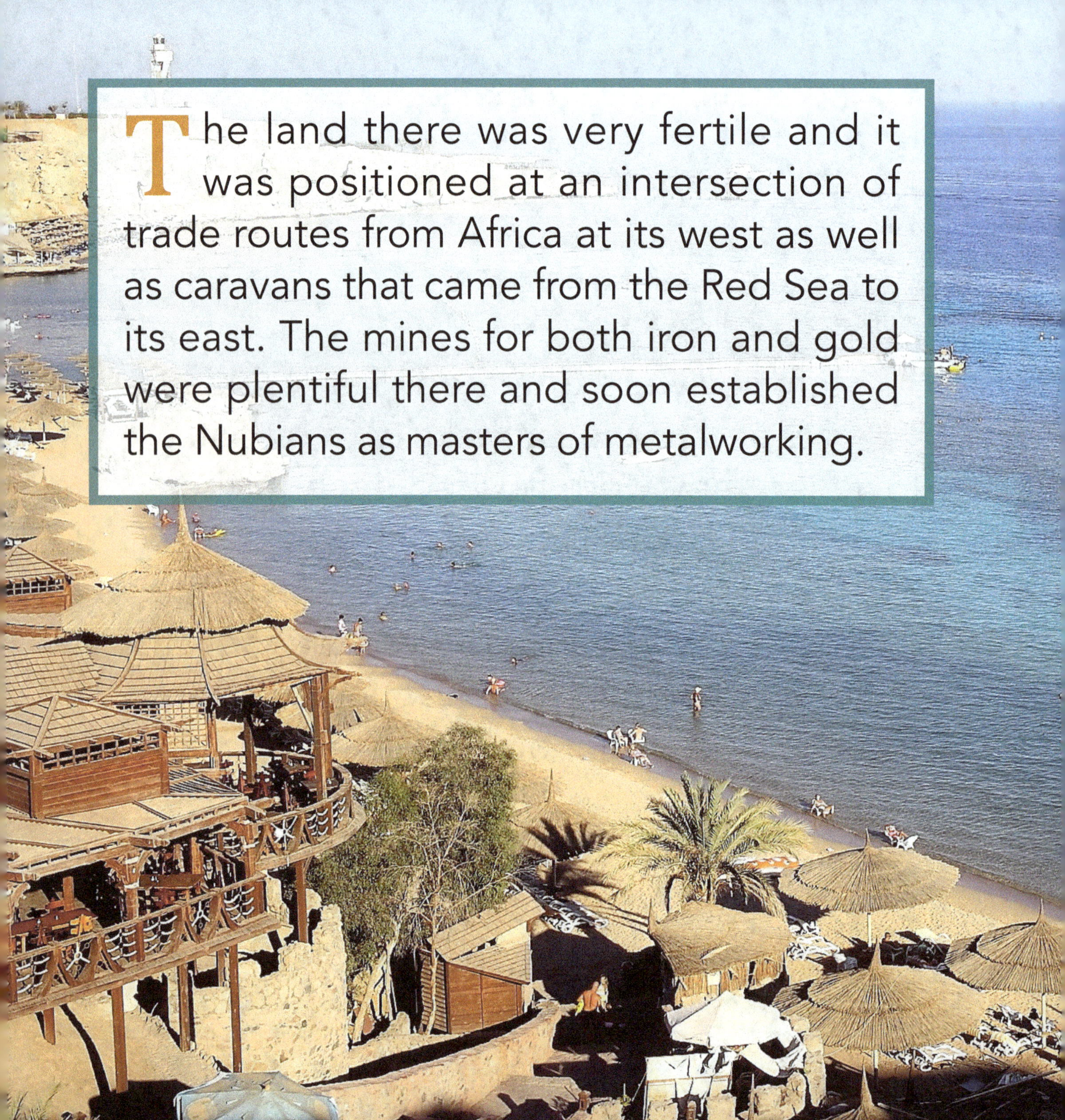

The land there was very fertile and it was positioned at an intersection of trade routes from Africa at its west as well as caravans that came from the Red Sea to its east. The mines for both iron and gold were plentiful there and soon established the Nubians as masters of metalworking.

RED SEA

A STATUE OF AMUN

THE ROYAL TOMBS

The Nubians, also called the Kushites, had religious beliefs and burial ceremonies that were similar to those of the Egyptians. Their burial rituals were influenced by religious rituals practiced by both the Egyptians and the Africans. Even after they had been pushed south, the Nubian kings were still buried at a burial site called Nuri, which was near their former capital city of Napata. Amun, one of the powerful Egyptian gods, was worshipped there.

Circa 250 BC, Meroë would become the preferred area for burials. There is a cemetery to the south of the city that was the first to have tombs and when it was full, a burial area was constructed further north. Today, this northern area still has some of the best pyramid ruins. There are majestic tombs there that were built for 30 kings and 8 queens.

MEROE PYRAMID

The first pyramids constructed in Meroë had stepped sides and the stones were set in place using a shaft that worked as a simple lever. Some archaeologists believe that the tops of these pyramids might have had cylindrical structures or spheres that haven't survived over time. By the third century AD, the pyramids constructed had smoother sides.

E ven though they were influenced by the architecture of the Egyptians, the Nubian pyramids in Meroë were smaller in size and didn't have sharply pointed capstones. Their pyramids resemble the Egyptian pyramids

that were built during the centuries earlier era of Egyptian history called New Kingdom from 1539 though 1075 BC. This earlier time period had a major impact on the culture of the Kushites.

On the eastern side of each pyramid, there were steps that led down to an entrance that was sealed off. Inside that sealed-up entrance there were large rooms underground that had vaulted ceilings. In some of the most ancient structures, the chambers for burial were decorated with illustrations from the Book of the Dead, the famous Egyptian burial "guidebook."

QUEEN AMANIRENAS OF MEROË

In its later history, the Nubian Kingdom had powerful queens. The term "Candace" was used to describe them. This title means "sister." Although the Kingdom of Kush was thriving for centuries, when Queen Cleopatra died in 30 BC things changed radically. Egypt became part of the Roman Empire.

QUEEN CLEOPATRA

At the beginning, the Kushites thought they had ensured their peace because they signed a treaty with the new Roman emperor Augustus.

Howomever, there were citizen tax revolts in the lands of Upper Egypt. Roman troops started to come into the lands further south that belonged to the Kushites. This was when the powerful one-eyed queen named Amanirenas took a stand.

ROMAN TROOPS

She had already lost her husband in battle and she was not about to lose her kingdom as well. She and her courageous forces

attacked the Romans at Aswan, which was the Roman's southern outpost. After that, their kingdom was left in peace.

The city of Meroë was uninhabited by the 4th century AD. Over time, information spread about the pyramids with their secret treasures. Robbers including Giuseppe Ferlini, the famous tomb robber, traveled there to raid the treasures.

When Ferlini brought these golden treasures to Europe in the 1830s, the Europeans realized that the mysterious Nubian culture had many of the same traditions as ancient Egypt.

SUMMARY

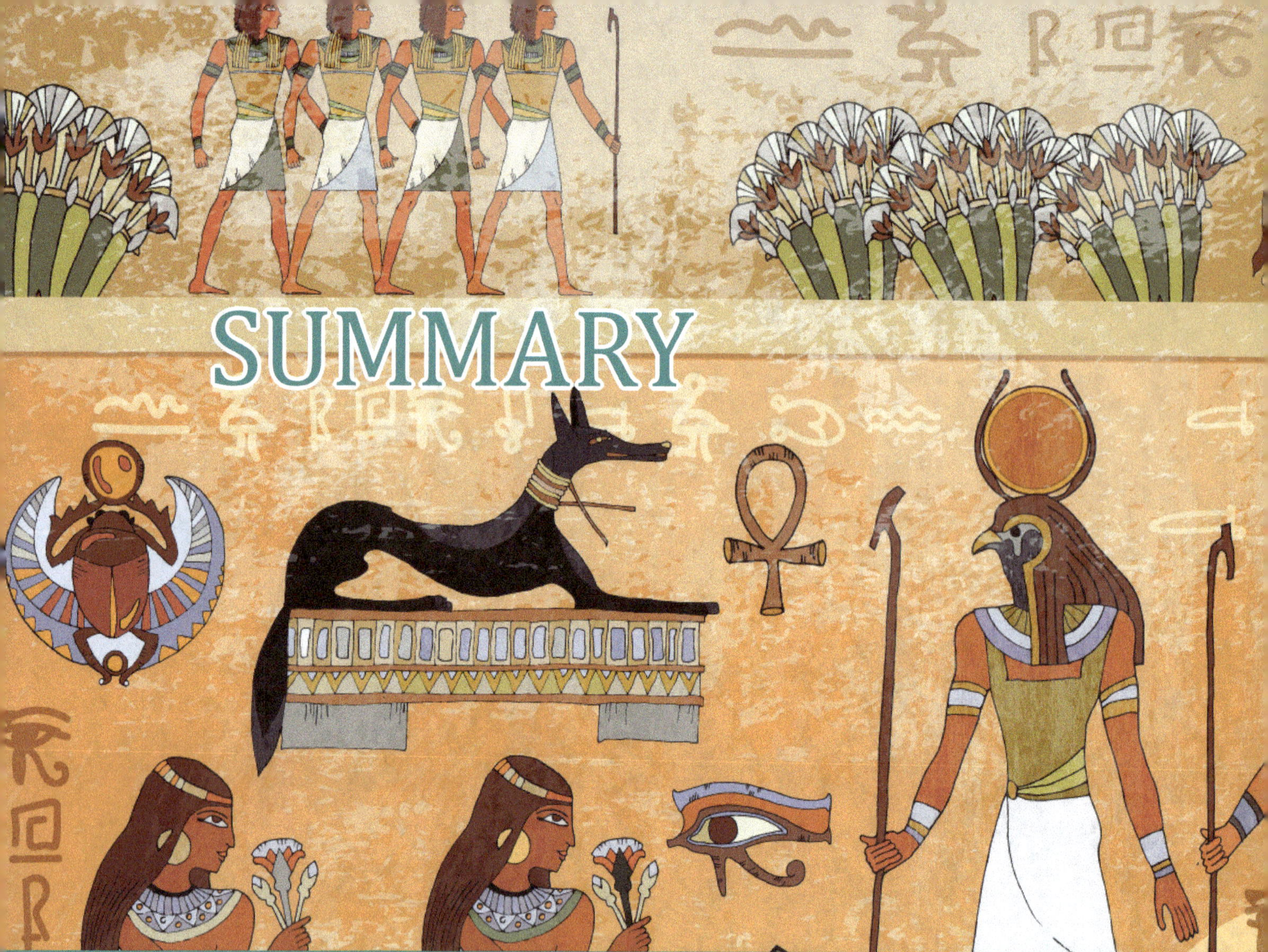

The Kingdom of Kush was established at the source of the Nile River before the Egyptian civilization was begun. There was fertile soil located there that wasn't dependent on the yearly floods that Egypt experienced.

For many centuries, the Kushites and Egyptians lived side by side. However, in 1500 BC, as Egypt expanded, they decided they wanted the Kingdom of Kush, with its prosperous gold and iron ore, to be part of their territories.

The Kushite culture was influenced by the Egyptians and in 730 BC, a powerful Nubian King named Piye took over Egypt. He was the first of the Black Pharaohs who ruled Egypt for 75 years. Eventually, the Kushites were driven further south when the Assyrians took over Egypt.

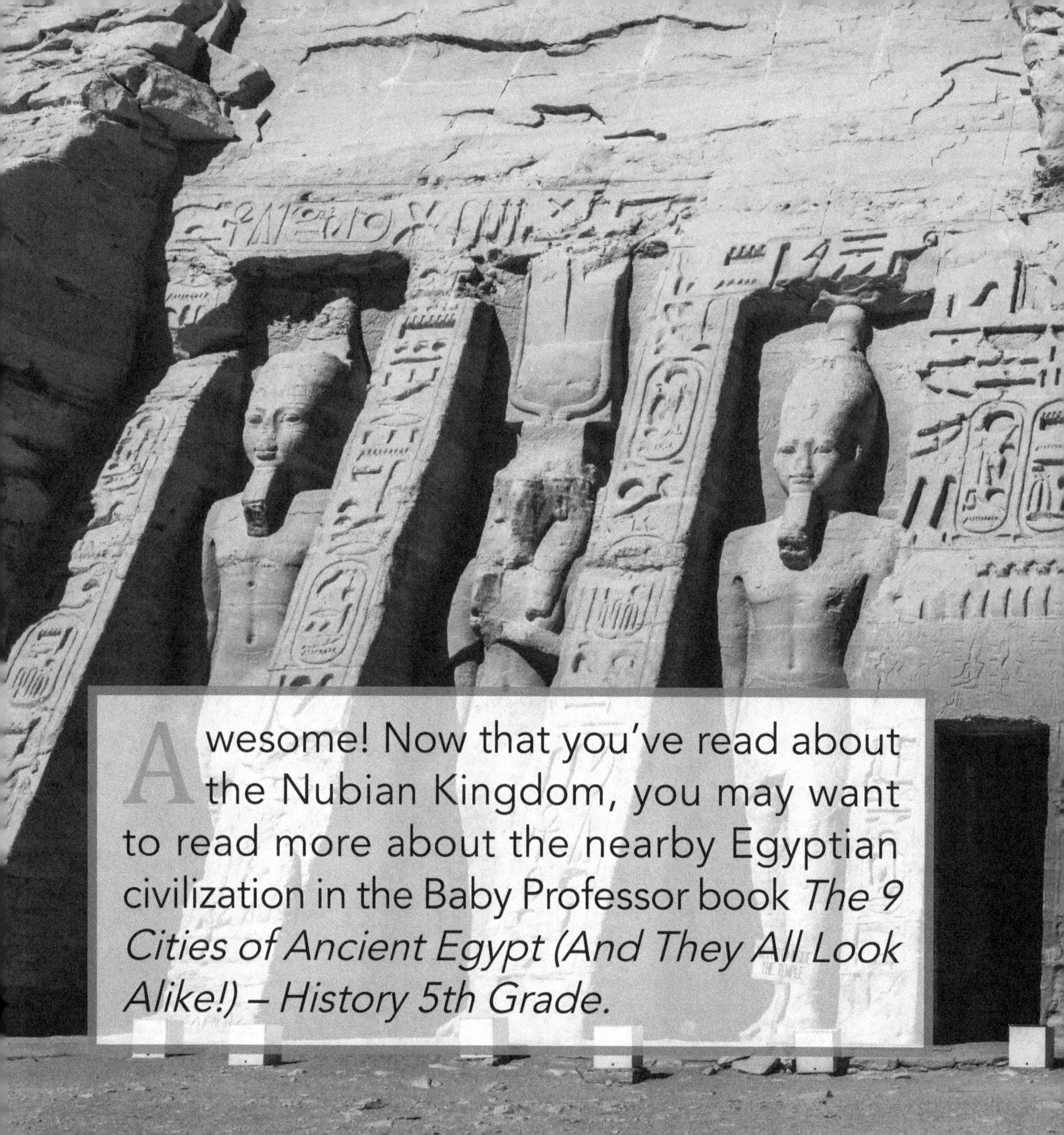

Awesome! Now that you've read about the Nubian Kingdom, you may want to read more about the nearby Egyptian civilization in the Baby Professor book *The 9 Cities of Ancient Egypt (And They All Look Alike!) – History 5th Grade*.

NO PHOTO INSIDE
THE TEMPLE

Visit
BABY PROFESSOR
EDUCATION KIDS
www.BabyProfessorBooks.com
to download Free Baby Professor eBooks
and view our catalog of new and exciting
Children's Books

www.ingramcontent.com/pod-product-compliance
Lightning Source LLC
Chambersburg PA
CBHW060615120726
48002CB00010B/2970